The Bible and African Americans

FACETS

We Read in the Bible and We Understan'

We read in the Bible and we understan'
That Samson was the strongest man
Samson went out at one time
And killed about a thousand Philistines.
Delilah fooled Samson, this we know
Because the Holy Bible tells us so.
She shaved off his head just as clean as your han',
And his strength became as any other man.

I heard a mighty rumbling under the groun'
It must be the devil running aroun'.
I heard a mighty rumbling up in the sky
It must be Jehovah passing by.
Jehovah sent down His chariot of fire
And carried Elijah up higher and higher.

Daniel was a Hebrew child
He went to pray to his God for a while
The king at once for Daniel did sen'
And he put him right down in the lion's den,
The Lord sent His angels the lions for to keep
And Daniel lay down and he went to sleep.

—*American Negro Songs and Spirituals,*
ed. John W. Work

the inspiration and challenge they have provided me during the last several years. And I deeply appreciate the generous financial support of the Ford Foundation. For the last several years, it has made possible the research project (African Americans and the Bible) and research resources that have helped me fine-tune and reframe the arguments that follow. Ford Foundation officer Constance H. Buchanan, in particular, has been an inspiration and a most valued conversation partner and critic, especially about what could be the broader social and cultural ramifications and political-educational implications of my scholarly work. I hope her challenge to me to put my arguments in popular form and Fortress Press's invitation to make this work a part of the Facets series, as they have come together in the work that follows, will prove to have been worth their efforts.

The Bible and African Americans

A Brief History

Vincent L. Wimbush

Fortress Press
Minneapolis

THE BIBLE AND AFRICAN AMERICANS
A Brief History

Cover image: Chain. Steve Cole/Getty Images. Used by
permission.
Cover and book design: Joseph P. Bonyata
Author photo by Michael Grimaldi.

ISBN: 0-8006-3574-4

Manufactured in the U.S.A.
07 06 05 04 03 1 2 3 4 5 6 7 8 9 10

For Mom
in love and gratitude

Contents

Acknowledgments

In this small volume, I have returned to the question of how African American engagement with the Bible can best be understood over its many centuries and radically diverse circumstances. I do so by revising and updating my earlier work in *Stony the Road We Trod: African American Biblical Interpretation* (Fortress Press, 1991). I want first to express my thanks to the Fund for Theological Education, Inc., for permission to publish the work that follows as a revised standalone volume.

Thanks are also due to the honest and constructive critics of the recent lectures I delivered that were the basis of my revisions: Professor Dieter Georgi and the

scholars, clergy, and students who partic-
ipated in the colloquium on the future of
biblical studies, near Frankfurt-am-Main,
Germany, in October 2001; Professor
Dennis Smith and the faculty, students,
alumni/ae, and clergy who attended the
Ministers' Week Conference sponsored by
Phillips Theological Seminary, Tulsa, Ok-
lahoma, in January 2001; Ms. Gertrude
Albert and the members of the Ridgewood Presbyterian Church, Ridgewood,
New Jersey, and their guests who attended the Lenten Lectures, March 2002;
Professor Frank Kirkland, Hunter College,
New York and the members of the Society
for the Study of African Philosophy who
attended the session held on March 17,
2002; and the Reverend Dr. Jay Rock of
the National Council of Churches and the
participants in the colloquium on Jewish
and Christian Dialogue who met in Stony
Point New York, April 15, 2002.

I owe a great deal to students in the
various degree programs and fields at
Union Theological Seminary and Columbia University and my New Testa-
ment/Early Christianity colleagues for

Introduction:
The Bible as Language-World

Think of the myriad ways in which the Bible daily intersects with African American culture. The preacher's lyrical enunciation of a passage from it forms the pretext for her Sunday morning sermon. Another preacher's use of excerpts from it is part of his class study of women's roles and codes of behavior in church and society. The youth's perfectly memorized recitation of it becomes part of special Sunday school exercises. The mass choir's moving and rhythmic representation of favorite stories from it forms jazzy gospel tunes. Its critical-prophetic stings are recalled by the lyrical jeremiads of the street preacher in the middle of the financial district. A carefully chosen anthology of passages from

it is distributed in leaflets to crowds try-
ing to negotiate the sidewalks along
125th Street in Harlem. The megaphone
blasting of certain passages from it
sounds a rhetorical cascade of denunciations of the world and of certain social
demographics in particular coursing
through Times Square. The hip-hop artist
interprets part of her dramatic life story
in terms parallel to one of its stories. It is
a source of healing and a predictor of
fates and fortunes in Spritualist churches.
The everyday glosses on passages from it,
the free invention of sayings and stories
and the imputation of such materials to it
occur in the barber shops, beauty parlors,
buses and subways, sports events, front
porches, bars and clubs, restaurants,
street corners. They provide persuasive
comments on the foibles, tragedies, para-
doxes, the successes and failures, the or-
dinariness and the extra-ordinariness of
life.

All these situations represent what may
be called points of cultural contact. They
represent encounters of various sorts between the people who have come to be

called African Americans and the collection of texts we have come to call the Bible. Recognition of the actual events through which a significant segment of African Americans originally came in contact with the Bible—within the framework of institutionalized domination (slavery) and at the hands of those who defined themselves in terms of the Book—makes cultural contact an appropriate description. Ongoing, dynamic, and in some cases even controversial, these encounters represent different types of practices among different groups in diverse settings. They raise numerous questions, here primarily historical. How did this fascinating situation develop? Why did the encounter persist over such a long period of time? How did African Americans come to this point of communicating so much to one another about one another and their views of the world in terms of the Bible—a text that the white dominants claimed to own? What changes and developments, what twists and turns characterize the encounter from its beginnings to now?

There can be no simple explanation for the long, intense, complex phenomenon of African American engagement with the Bible. In the setting that was understood to be the partly biblically inspired, violently secured "New World"—the "New Israel" that would become the United States—the Bible was the single most important centering object for social identity and orientation among European dominants. So it should not occasion surprise that the Bible would come to be seen by enslaved and otherwise dominated Africans in this setting as an important object. It quickly came to function as a language-world, the storehouse of rhetorics, images, and stories that, through a complex history of engagements, helped establish African Americans as *a circle of the biblical imaginary*.[1] It helped a people imagine themselves as something other, in another world, different from what their immediate situation reflected or demanded.

The experience of being uprooted from their African homelands and forced to labor in a strange place produced in the

first African slaves a type of disorientation.[2] This disorientation, contrived by
the white slavers because of its advantages for them, was most evident in
language and communication. Although
Africans from the same social groups and
homelands who were captured and enslaved could have communicated with
one another without problem, the slavers
took steps to frustrate communication.
Being so deprived initially of a language
through which meaningful communication could be realized, and cut off from
their roots, including their languages and
religious heritage, the first African slaves
experienced a type of "social death."[3]
That is what slavery was supposed to
mean in the eyes of many. Part of what
came to be the Europeans' and Euramericans' justification for the enslavement
of Africans was the "strangeness" and
inferiority of the latter—their physical
attributes and their culture, especially
their languages.[4] Given this view, but
also, ironically, given the threat that the
Africans always posed in the minds of
many white dominants, frustrating,

scrambling, or altogether undermining communications among Africans was part of the slavers' ideology and an ongoing stratagem of domination. Among Europeans, Euramericans, and, as the cultural contact continued and intensified and became more complex, also among many Africans, it was understood that part of what it meant to be fully enslaved was to be cut off from one's cultural roots, to be without a language with which to demonstrate one's humanity.

But this state of affairs did not always prevail even for the African slaves. A great many of the slaves did adopt—as part of the complex phenomenon of acquiring a number of new skills, symbols, and languages for survival—the Bible as a kind of "language" through which they negotiated both the strange new world called America and their slave existence. With this language they began to wax eloquent not only with the white slavers and not only among themselves, but also about themselves, about the ways in which they understood their situation in America—as slaves, as freed persons, as disenfranchised persons, as a people. For the great majority of African Americans, the Bible has historically functioned not merely to reflect and legitimize piety (narrowly understood), but as a language-world full of stories—of heroes and heroines, of heroic peoples and their pathos and victory, sorrow and joy, sojourn and fulfillment. In short, the Bible became a "world" into which African Americans could retreat, a world they could identify with, draw strength from, and, in fact, manipulate for self-affirmation. This coming into language is, I think, a reasonable and compelling initial explanation for the types of contemporary encounters described above.

But what warrants further investigation is the peoples' use of the Bible as a language, even a language-world. Nearly all interpreters have acknowledged that the Bible has played an important role in the history of African Americans. What remains is a comprehensive effort to relate and then interpret that history through the various major types of engagements with the Bible by African

Americans. This short work is an attempt
to provide a working outline of such a
history. Its importance lies in its sugges-
tiveness, its heuristic value, its challenge
and inspiration for further serious reflection and research, not its comprehensive-
ness. It is no more than a summary of
what I see as the major types of "readings" of the Bible among African Americans within or in relationship to various
"circles" (or shapes and conditions) of social formation from their introduction to
it during slavery up to the modern period. The types of readings actually correspond to different historical periods
and are meant to reflect different responses to historical (social, political,
economic) situations and collective self-
understandings. At the beginning, several clarifying statements are in order.

First, each historical "reading" is assumed to be public, or communal, not
private or individualistic. I attempt here
to trace broad, well-recognized social
movements, practices, and sensibilities.
Second, each reading is assumed to have
emerged out of particular historical life-

settings and to have been evidenced and preserved in different types of historical sources—for example, songs, sermons, rituals, testimonies, books, pamphlets, political and other types of speeches and addresses, and everyday communications in everyday situations. Third, each type of reading is assumed not to be in evidence solely in terms of the direct quotation of certain biblical passages—although the occurrence of certain passages over and over again would obviously be significant—but in terms of a wide range of approaches to the texts. Our emphasis will not be on interpreting the content of the Bible but on discerning the Bible's *social functions* in historical African American communities. Fourth, although this work is divided according to types of readings, the predominant orientation and method are social-historical, cultural-historical, and ethnological. They are best understood in this way. The ultimate goal is to provide the framework for a different kind of *interpretive history* of African Americans—based not on great individuals or prestigious institutions, but on the peoples' interpretations or sensibilities and orientations as evidenced in their engagements with the most important, most accessible, and most influential text in our culture.

Even as each type of reading represents a distinct period in the history of African Americans, the types of readings are not strictly chronological—no one reading completely disappears when another begins. There is much overlap in readings of different historical periods. One period differs from another in emphasis. So, given the kind of historical inquiry this book represents, strict chronological boundaries that correspond with the different types of readings would not be helpful; they could in fact serve only to frustrate a main thesis of this work—that there is much overlap and fluidity between readings. Our chronological markers will be general. Finally, although I make necessary reference to a collective, African Americans, I do not assume that all persons of African descent in the United States are necessarily included in the historical outline provided. It is enough for my purposes to show that some persons or a significant portion of the populations are to be included.

Reading 1

African Sensibilities as the Center of the Circle: First Contact

The interaction between African Americans and the Bible should begin not with their involuntary arrival in the New World as slaves but with their contact, as far back as the fifteenth century, with Europeans on African soil. The interests and motives of the European explorers, merchants, sailors, and missionaries who traveled to western, central, and southern Africa were mixed from the beginning. Their direct or indirect efforts to "convert" Africans to various forms of Christianity could not ultimately be separated from their attempts to exploit them commercially, to dominate them, and then to humanize and socialize (make European) them—Africans, who were deemed first different, then inferior.[5]

And the Bible? The book interchangeably referred to as "The Bible," "The Word of God," "The Scriptures," was a most important part of the European missionaries' religious-cultural self-understandings, their self-presentations, and their ideological and propaganda offensives. They understand the Bible, referred to in code or freighted abbreviation, to be God's direct word to and for and about them. But it was really a mirror-reflection of their own world, or the world they constructed and dominated. In the Book, it was claimed, were God's mandates regarding world order and domination to those who now discovered and named themselves specifically as *white European Christians*. In the Book they could see themselves over against the white-European-discovered and European-named *other—the Black African pagans, barbarians, savages, infidels*. This occurred despite all the internal variety, differentiation, and divisions among Black Africans. The Book belonged to the Europeans to interpret; it was theirs as a socializing agent, as a cultural road map, as a discursive framework, and as an ideological mandate for practices of domination. It was theirs as a weapon.[6]

Hard to miss, as part of the external possessions of those who came among them as dominating people, was the book that explained and guaranteed their overall power situation in the world. How could the Europeans' Bible have been deemed by the Africans as anything other than the most special of cultural-ideological cargo among the many items and kinds of cargo that the Europeans brought with them to various parts of the African continent? How could such sacred cargo be responded to among Africans except as a compelling and dangerous power, as something that should be approached and engaged warily? Under the historical circumstances of initial contact, how could the Bible be understood in the minds of both Europeans and Africans as anything other than European sacred cargo?[7]

The evidence—mainly, although not exclusively, from Europeans—suggests that it was the sacred book as cargo that was most often the primary object of exchange. It was also the source of provocation, challenge, and confusion for both sides of the initial cultural contact.[8] It was the Bible, after all, that most dramatically symbolized for the parties concerned the claimed power and advantages of the Europeans. Beyond the incarnation of Jesus, the Bible was claimed by the European Christians to be the highest and most compelling revelation of transcendence— the most secure bridge between the divine and the worldly. It was God's "word." Odd as it seems, impossible though it be to explain, it was just the fateful twists and turns of history or divine providence that the "word" happened *to* Europeans, *in* European languages, *through* European traditions, and institutions. Europeans had never thought to ponder or explain this.

So how did Africans generally react in their first contact with the Bible as the strangest and most important item among the many in the Europeans' cargo? With a mixture of awe and respect, befuddlement and contempt. They reacted with awe and respect because the Bible as cargo was obviously and rightly identified with the Europeans, who even before they began their domination of Africans—and aside from what other cargo they brought along—must have seemed strange on account of their differences—in appearance, in speech, and in their ways. They were considered to be other in the world called Africa. And they were assumed to be powerful simply by virtue of their having appeared and having traveled from another world. A perception of power was associated with simply being able to show up from another world.

Constant references to and engagement with the Bible by missionaries, particularly as the single and ultimate authority, were not lost on Africans. Missionary claims about the Bible as the locus of the sacred evoked a certain amount of respect and awe. The claim that the sacred was located in a book was no doubt thought at first to have been odd: only someone thoroughly socialized in a culture of the (sacred) book, whether in the east or the west, could think of the textualization of divine communication as anything other than odd. Humankind had not always or even primarily thought of revelation in terms of a book.[9]

But it was not necessarily the claim that the sacred could be located in a book or understood in relationship to a book that was the problem for Africans. Since the sacred was thought by Africans to pervade everything, why, odd as it may have seemed for most Africans, could not revelation come to be understood in relationship with a book? Such acceptance was evidence of the traditional African sensibility, in particular its openness to and acceptance of the possibility of discovering and engaging the sacred almost everywhere and on differing terms. No, it was not the European notion of the sacred book in itself that was most problematic for Africans. It was instead the Europeans' claims regarding the *boundedness* and the *exclusive* authority of the book and their emphasis on the *past* and on the *discontinuous,* or single, nature of the revelation associated with the book.[10]

So, among many Africans whom the Europeans attempted to missionize, an initial reaction of respect and awe gave way to befuddlement and contempt. Seventeenth-century Dutch Lutheran pastor Wilhelm Johann Mueller's obviously defensive observation about the Fetu peoples on the Gold Coast illustrates these reactions. It is compelling in its registration of the conflicting epistemologies and worldviews:

> They do not desire to believe in the Almighty Creator of Heaven and Earth, let alone fear, love and have faith in Him. . . . If one talks to them of God's miracles and gracious works . . . some of them listen in amazement, but most scoff. If one tells them of the wonders which God performed long ago in the Old Testament, they immediately ask how many years ago it was that such wonders occurred—as if to say, "If such a long time has passed, how can one actually know such things?"[11]

Oddly enough, befuddlement and contempt worked both ways: they were felt among Africans and Europeans—missionaries, merchants, and other contact groups—in Africa and the New World. The Africans' reactions to the claims of the Europeans about their book in turn provoked the same emotions among Europeans. This situation almost seemed to define modern culture shock and culture confrontation.[12] Neither culture groups could, in this early period of contact, understand and penetrate the others' worldviews. Many Africans could not understand how revelation could be limited to a book and only to a particular book and the past situations about which it "spoke." As for the Europeans, most found it incredible and exasperating that Africans could not understand Europeans' self-evident, self-referential claims about the Bible and engage them and it on terms and bases that they had modeled and communicated.

Reflected in circumstances that often represented African cultural parity, if not superiority, and only foreshadowings of straightforward European positions of superiority, the first-stage African reactions to the Bible were not only the strongest critiques of European ways and claims to power but also the most culturally and ideologically critical reactions that Africans would ever register. With the mixed or even negative first-stage reaction to the European wielding of the Bible, a deep divide—a certain kind of clash of worldviews—occurred.

This could have resulted in the end of the story, end of rapprochement, end of contact and engagement with the Bible. So one would have thought, and to many Africans and a few Europeans it must have seemed likely. But what actually followed were beginnings of widespread and intense contact, the shape of which was greatly, although not entirely, determined by European domination. As the modern Europeans and Americans trafficking in Africans slaves entered the picture on a large scale, the relations between Africans and Europeans obviously took a radically different and tragic turn. This fateful turn is reflected rather sharply in the history of the conjuncture of the Bible and African Americans.

Reading 2

Creating the "New World" Circle: Folk Culture

From the first reading to the second reading, the setting changes from Africa to the North Atlantic worlds, more specifically, in terms of our focus, to what has become the United States. For almost all those of African background, the new setting meant slavery. This was the harsh reality from the beginning of the European settlements in the early seventeenth century to emancipation in the mid-nineteenth. So although already a forced presence in the United States, it was well into the eighteenth century that Africans began to "convert" to Christianity in significant numbers, significant enough to justify labeling this period the beginning of a type of African American folk religious ethos. On plantations and in camp meetings the Black enslaved came to respond to the Europeans' evangelical preaching and piety, especially to their emphasis on conversion experience as the sign of God's acceptance of the worth of the individual, and to the often spontaneous formation of communities of the converted for fellowship and mutual affirmation. Because testimony regarding personal experience with God was claimed to be the single most important criterion for entry into the evangelical communities—relativizing, though not obliterating, social status and racial identification—and because that criterion held the promise of a degree of egalitarianism and affirmation, it was no wonder that the Africans began to respond in great numbers to the evangelicals, especially the white Methodists and Baptists.[13]

Sacralization of the Bible among white evangelical Protestants, north and south, could hardly have been ignored by the Africans. The young nation officially defined itself as a "biblical nation"; indeed, popular culture was thoroughly biblical.[14] It would have been difficult not to take

note of the diversity of views that reading the Bible could inspire, not only between north and south as cultural,
political readings, but also among evangelical communities. The lesson that the
Africans learned from these evangelicals
was not only that faith was to be interpreted in light of reading the Bible, but
also that each person had freedom in interpreting the Bible. Given differences
between individuals and different religious groups, the Africans learned that
they, too, could read the Book freely.
They could read certain parts and ignore
others. They could and did articulate
their interpretations in their own way—in
songs, prayers, sermons, rituals, dance,
testimonies, and addresses. So the Book
came to represent a virtual language-
world that the enslaved folk, too, could
enter and manipulate in light of their social experiences. After all, everyone
could approach the Bible under the guid-
ance of the Spirit, that is, in his or her
own way.[15]

And interpret they did. They were attracted primarily to stories—those about

the adventures of the Hebrews in bondage and escaping from bondage, and those about the wondrous works, compassion, passion, and resurrection of Jesus. But they were also attracted to the oracles and prophecies, especially the prophetic denunciations of social injustice and the visions of social justice. With these and other texts, the mostly enslaved African American "Christians" created a circle—of social solidarity based upon entry into a language-world that was biblical. In their spirituals and in their sermons and testimonies, African Americans interpreted the Bible in light of their experiences. Faith became identification with the heroes and heroines of the Hebrew Bible and with the long-suffering but ultimately victorious Jesus. As the people of God in the Hebrew Bible were once delivered from enslavement, so, in the future, the Africans sang and shouted, would they. As Jesus suffered unjustly but was raised from the dead to new life, so, they sang, would they be "raised" from their "social death" to new life. So went the songs, sermons, and testimonies.

The spirituals reflect the process of trans-
forming the book religion of the dominant peoples into the necessarily more
complex renderings of perspectives and
sentiments of the Africans who were
made slaves:

> Go down, Moses
> Way down in Egypt land,
> Tell ole Pharaoh,
> Let my people go.

> Dey crucified my Lord,
> An' He never said a mumblin' word.
> Dey crucified my Lord,
> An' He never said a mumblin' word,
> Not a word—not a word—not a word.

> Dey nailed Him to de tree,
> An' He never said a mumblin' word.
> Day nailed Him to de tree,
> An' He never said a mumblin' word,
> Not a word—not a word—not a word.

> Dey pierced Him in de side,
> An' He never said a mumblin' word.

Dey pierced Him in de side,
An' He never said a mumblin' word,
Not a word—not a word—not a word.

Sometimes I feel like a motherless child,
Sometimes I feel like a motherless child,
Sometimes I feel like a motherless child,
A long ways from home.

In his classic collection and interpretation of the spirituals, James Weldon Johnson captures well the importance of the Bible in the imaginations of the African American religious folk experience that extends from the period of slavery to the present:

At the psychic moment there was at hand the precise religion for the condition in which [the African] found himself thrust. Far from . . . his native land and customs, despised by those among whom he lived, experiencing the pang of separation of loved ones on the auction block . . . [the African] seized Christianity, . . . the religion which implied the hope that in the next world there would be a reversal of conditions. . . . The result was a body of songs voicing all the cardinal virtues of Christianity . . . through a modified form of primitive African music. . . . [The African] took complete refuge in Christianity, and the Spirituals were literally forged in the heat of religious fervor. . . . It is not possible to estimate the sustaining influence that the story of the Jews as related in the Old Testament exerted upon the Negro. This story at once caught and fired the imaginations of the Negro bards, and they sang, sang their hungry listeners into a firm faith.[16]

Johnson's interpretation of the function of African American religion as the "other-worldly" religion of oppressed peoples has been significantly modified by more recent social-scientific research of religion in general[17] and on African Americans religion in particular.[18] But very few interpreters of African American history, from whatever methodological perspective, have captured and articulated so well the importance of the Bible in the imagination of African Americans.

The spirituals and other songs and forms of representation reflect an approach to biblical interpretation informed by trauma—both physical and psychosocial. Interpretation was in almost all cases not controlled by the literal words of the texts because the texts were, for a number of reasons, *heard* (and touched and otherwise experienced) more than simply *read*. They were engaged as stories that seized and freed the imagination. Rather than an end in itself, interpretation seemed actually to have been understood and experienced as the collective freed consciousness and imagination of the African slaves (and the generations to follow) as they heard the biblical stories and retold them to reflect their own actual social situations, as well as their visions for a different world order.[19]

Many of the biblical stories, themselves the product of ancient cultures with well-established oral traditions, functioned sometimes as allegory, as parable, or as veiled social criticism. Such stories served the Africans well, not only on account of their well-established oral traditions, but also because their situation dictated indirect social criticism—what Zora Neale Hurston referred to as "hitting a straight lick with a crooked stick."[20] The use of the Bible within the circle of the African American "folk," coursing through but also well beyond the period of slavery and extending into the present in the United States, is characterized by a nonliteralist looseness, a multilayered, multisensory engagement and even a playfulness—sometimes within but often beyond what became the strictly church-defined interests and functions. So even the stories that were understood to constitute the Bible were manipulated, as Hurston made clear, to "suit our vivid imagination," that is, to help create a language-world, a *circle* for the expression of the ways, experiences, perspectives, and hopes of the folk.[21]

Such a circle was created not alone but certainly in primary and dynamic relationship to the Bible. The engagement of the Bible was in African American folk culture understood in terms of seeking the "hidden" or "inside meanin' of words" that held the key to the enigma of existence characterized by slavery, racial discrimination, inequality, and violence.[22] For African Americans, the power to crack the codes of the Bible was also the power to negotiate, even overcome, the opposition of the world. Whether "dressed"[23] or "visited"[24] by the spirit, whether read backwards in order to ward off ghosts or in a totally random way in order to tell fortunes,[25] whether used in cures or conjuration,[26] the Bible was understood by the folk to be a special medium of communication about life challenges and enigmas as well as a power to deal with them.

Originating in the period of slavery, this folk "reading" of the Bible was complex, dynamic, and fluid. It was ever changing in order to help create and give voice to a people and help them negotiate changes in the nonetheless always hostile world. The fluidity, complexity, and diversity of the folk circle made it necessarily the most popular circle. It was in these terms also foundational: most if not all other African American readings to come would in some sense be built upon and judged against it. The folk circle reflects what arguably has been so basic to the orientation of the majority of African Americans that all subsequent debates about orientation, worldview, and strategies for survival or liberation have begun with this period and what it represents. In sum, it represents Africans' pragmatic, relative accommodation to existence in America. It is pragmatic because it attempts to come to grips with what resources, sources of power and opportunities were at hand for survival and amelioration of psychosocial status; relative because it never assumed that persons of African descent could ever be fully integrated into American society.

The Bible was clearly understood as one of the cultural resources at hand. The loose, sometimes playful, sometimes principled, "not-reading," multiform engagement of the biblical text was a complex reflection of the relative acceptance of dominant cultural values, not a mere reflection of functional illiteracy.[27]

This second reading is hermeneutically and socially critical. It reflects the fact that the Bible, understood as the "white folks'" book, was accepted but not interpreted in the way that white Christians and the dominant culture in general interpreted it. So America's biblical culture was accepted by the Africans, but not in the way white Americans accepted it or in the way the whites preferred that others accept it.

Reading 3

Establishing the Circle: National(ist) Identities and Formations

In the northern states during the decades preceding the Civil War, persons of African descent were in degrees and numbers less enslaved than their southern counterparts. A few were "allowed" some opportunities to educate themselves both formally and informally. Fewer still were those who could even seriously imagine themselves enjoying the opportunities and responsibilities of free citizenship. Notwithstanding the northern states' hypocrisy, inconsistencies, and ironic limitations regarding "freedom" for persons of African descent during this period, it is clear that these states were for the most part environments in which "Africans" could openly begin to cultivate and develop ideas, arguments, and strategies for action that would address their plight and those of their enslaved brothers and sisters.

In the early to middle decades of the nineteenth century, articulate persons of African descent—exhorters, clerics, writers, organizers of all types, primarily but not exclusively in the North—held forth in public and joined the national debate regarding many issues, the most important of which had to do with the morality, social utility, economics, and politics of slavery. Because the matter of slavery was such a controversial national issue—cutting to the heart of national identity—the extent to which such persons joined the public debates about slavery also partly reflected and partly laid the foundations for varieties of Black "national" consciousness and formations. I suggest that the impetus, force, and agenda of such consciousness and formations can be understood in terms of "readings" of the Bible. Such readings should be associated with a wide range of differences in consciousness, political orientations, and contexts or domains—from churches and other religious associations (local, regional, and protonational), to schools, a variety of social and cultural organizations, political parties, and governmental offices and departments. In terms of political strategies, orientations, and consciousness, the differences ranged from strict accommodationists and integrationists to the most radical Black nationalists. The consistent thread was the national public nature of the debate, the different voices and stances that contributed to the making of what is now recognized as African America.[28]

In the religious domains of the early- and mid-nineteenth century, local congregations and other local and regional and protonational denominational bodies developed among African Americans that were independent of white control.[29] What followed from this development were representations of the oppositional (that is, primarily antiracist) character and agenda of the now-dominant religious culture developed by African Americans.[30] Sermons, orations, exhortations, and addresses crafted by self-styled converted Christian slaves and freed persons—whether formally ordained or formally trained in theology—reflected concern about the evils of slavery, the social lot of Africans in America. What is striking is that both the explanation for the social situation of the Africans and the solution to their problems were cast in biblical language.

Since colonial days, white Americans had been familiar with reading the Bible from a nationalist perspective. The story of the Hebrews' long struggle to come into possession of the Promised Land was a paradigm for the Europeans' struggles to come into possession of the American "Promised Land." In the nineteenth century, African Americans began to hold forth against such typological claims of white Protestant Americans. African Americans pointed out that their own experience in the New World was an antitype of the ancient Hebrews' experience with respect to Palestine.[31] This they did by applying their favorite biblical passages to an array of social issues—in sermons, prayers, official denominational addresses, creeds, and mottos. Black freedom fighters waxed biblical about the kinship of all of humanity under the sovereignty of the one God, about slavery as a base evil in opposition to the will of God, about the imperatives of the teachings of Jesus to make all nations a part of God's reign, and about the judgment that is to be leveled against all those—including slavers—who frustrate God's will on earth.[32]

The preoccupation of many African American orators with the theme of Christian radical inclusion can be seen most strikingly in the engagement of one of the New Testament passages they found resonant and compelling. The key passage to Christian moral and social ethical thinking and practice was "There is neither Jew nor Greek, there is neither slave nor free, there is neither male nor female; for you are all one in Christ Jesus" (Gal. 3:28). Ironically, this biblical verse, which stresses the principle of Christian unity, was embraced and referred to over and over again even as the

African-independent or separate-church movements got under way. This passage and other passages were used to level prophetic judgment against a society that thought of itself as biblical in its foundation and ethic.

This reading of the Bible among African Americans extends at least from the nineteenth century to the present. It has historically reflected and shaped the ethos and thinking of the majority of African Americans. If the second reading—an interpretation of the earliest period of enslavement and beyond—represents the creation of the circle of reference (vis-à-vis the Bible), then this third reading—an interpretation of the nineteenth century and beyond—fixed the nature and circumference of the circle. It was the period of self-conscious articulation, consolidation, and institutionalization.

From the nineteenth century into the present, the ideal of the kinship and unity of all humanity under the sovereignty of God has been important to a great number of African Americans, as reflected in the official mottos and pronouncements of the independent denominations. Two examples will help to demonstrate this.

At the twentieth quadrennial session of the General Conference of the African Methodist Episcopal Church (May 1896) the saying of Bishop Daniel Payne, "God our Father; Christ our Redeemer; Man our Brother," became the official motto of the denomination:

> This is the official motto of the A.M.E. Church, and her mission in the commonwealth of Christianity is to bring all denominations and races to acknowledge and practice the sentiments contained therein. When these sentiments are universal in theory and practice, then the mission of the distinctive colored organizations will cease.[33]

In his presidential address before the forty-second annual session of the National Baptist Convention, in December 1922, Dr. E. C. Morris specified how Afro-Baptists understood and justified their separate existence:

> We early imbibed the religion of the white man; we believed in it; we believe in it now. . . . But if that religion does not mean what it says, if God did not make of one blood all nations of men to dwell on the face of the earth, and if we are not to be counted as part of that generation, by those who handed the oracle down to us, the sooner we abandon them or it, the sooner we will find our place in a religious sect in the world.[34]

The reading of the Bible in evidence here can be characterized as prophetic nationalism that could range from apologetics to radicalism. By this I mean that African Americans used the Bible to make self-assertive claims against a racist America that claimed to be a biblical nation. African Americans were clamoring for realization of the principles of inclusion, equality, and kinship that they understood the Bible to mandate. Beginning in the nineteenth century and extending into the twentieth, African Americans consistently and systematically attempted to make use of the Bible to force "biblical" America to honor biblical principles. The very fact that the Bible was read in this way revealed African Americans' orientation and collective self-understanding—they desired to be integrated into American society. Their critical, polemical, and race- and culture-conscious reading of the Bible reflected their desire to enter the mainstream of American society. For many, perhaps most, African Americans, the Bible itself came to represent American society itself. A critical reading of the Bible was thought to be a critical reading of American society. That the Bible—and the whole of the tradition of which it was a signal part—was engaged at all signified relative acceptance of American society.

Irony must be seen in the fact that it was from the situation of institutional separatism that the prophetic call went out for the realization of the biblical principles of universalism, equality, and the kinship of all humanity. Perhaps African Americans had begun to see the inevitability of America's irony: the call for oneness could be made only apart from others, lest particularity be lost; but since particularity in America often meant being left out or discriminated against, exhortation for inclusion was made.

There were, of course, organizers and leaders, writers and orators who operated outside of, if not in opposition to, even the separate and strictly religious domain during this period. But focus on the engagement with the Bible in American history allows us to see how questionable our assumption of a separate religious domain is. The long, intense African American engagement with the Bible scrambles or belies such separation. What the African American story suggests instead is the need for respect for the wide range of different orientations.

Frederick Douglass stands as one eloquent example of a nineteenth-century interpreter of the Bible who took the interpretive principle of the kinship of humanity under the sovereignty of God and applied it to the emancipation agenda. Along with many others he was eloquent in his excoriations of "Christian" and "biblical" America:

> The Christianity of America is a Christianity, of whose votaries it may be as truly said, as it was of the ancient scribes and Pharisees, "They bind heavy burdens, and grievous to be borne, and lay them on men's shoulders, but they themselves will not move them with one of their fingers. All their works they do for to be seen of men." . . . Dark and terrible as is this picture, I hold it to be strictly true of the overwhelming mass of professed Christians of America. . . . They would be shocked at the proposition of fellowshipping a sheep-stealer; and at the same time they hug to their communion a man-stealer, and brand me an infidel, if I find fault with them for it. They attend with Pharisaical strictness to the outward forms of religion, and at the same time neglect the weightier matters of law, judgment, mercy, and faith.[35]

Others, of course, were associated with even more radical "Black nationalist" rhetoric and agenda. Their uses of the Bible reflected this agenda through their interpretations of history, their perspectives on ancient and current societal ideals, and their calls for independence, self-reliance, and self-governance. David Walker's words can be read in this way.

> All persons who are acquainted with history, and particularly the Bible . . . are willing to admit that God made man to serve Him alone . . . that God Almighty is the sole proprietor or master of the *whole* human family. . . . [This] God will not suffer us, always to be oppressed. Our sufferings will come to an end, in spite of all the Americans this side of eternity. Then we will want all the learning and talents among ourselves, and perhaps more, to govern ourselves.— 'Every dog must have its day,' the American's is coming to an end.[36]

Maria W. Stewart, one of first female African American public speakers, can also be read as a prophetic nationalist. Having been informed of efforts on the part of the Colonization Society to form an association of young men to encourage those of African descent in the United States descent to go to Liberia, she blasted the colonizationists and challenged Africans through prophetic and apocalyptic imagery and rhetoric:

It appears to me that America has become like the great city of Babylon, for she has boasted in her heart: "I sit a queen and am no widow, and shall see no sorrow!" She is, indeed, a seller of slaves and the souls of men; she has made the Africans drunk with the wine of fornication; she has put them completely beneath her feet. . . . But many powerful sons and daughters of Africa will shortly arise, who will put down vice and immorality among us, and declare by Him that sitteth upon the throne that they will have their rights; and if refused, I am afraid they will spread horror and devastation around. I believe that the oppression of injured Africa has come up before the majesty of Heaven. . . . The unfriendly whites . . . would drive us to a strange land, but before I go the bayonet shall pierce me through. . . .[37]

Reading 4

Reshaping the Circle: Re-mixes and Re-formations

This fourth reading of the Bible has its origins in the large urban areas of the early twentieth century. It continues to have great influence in the present. Included here are a number of groups with little or no formal ties to one another. What they have in common, however, is a compelling interest in "re-mixing" (to use the language of contemporary pop music) or re-formulating traditional forms. The fundamental precipitant for this interest lies in the social situation faced by the great majority of African Americans in the early decades of the twentieth century. In the years after World War I most African Americans lived in the rural areas and small towns of the south. Some had vivid memories of the pain of slavery. All had continuing experiences of the south's postslavery system of social and economic and legal apartheid. Many also experienced physical brutality.

Beginning in the period after the First World War and extending beyond the period of the Second World War, African Americans were associated with one of the most dramatic phenomena in the modern period—mass migration to the cities of the north, south, and west. As nations, including the United States, waged wars, altered state boundaries, and resettled peoples on a grand scale throughout Europe, and as the wars brought on social and economic rearrangements, masses of African Americans made their own moves to write their history and to change the condition of their own lives. Responding to some direct calls for workers, but mostly because of word of mouth and rumors about job opportunities in factories and shipyards in the large cities, the masses moved with courage, determination, and hope. They moved to remake their lives, to reshape them.[38]

To get a sense of some of the ramifications of the migrations, great personalities and institutions might be focused upon. But the masses themselves provide clearer and more dramatic evidence of what was at issue and what was wrought. The Black masses in this period created new religious formations, such as Holiness, Pentecostal, and many others, intended to re-form the old. They represented responses to the challenges of the new worlds—the urban settings. Once again, focusing on the ways in which the Bible was engaged illuminates their orientation and deep-seated views.

Attitudes toward and uses of the Bible and other sacred texts open a window onto some points of commonality of these new religious movements. These new groups tended to develop esoteric knowledge or principles of interpretation of the socioreligiously authorized Protestant or Catholic Bible; to lay claim to the absolute legitimacy of such knowledge or principles; to claim exclusive possession and knowledge of other holy books, or previously apocryphal parts of the Bible;

to claim to have in their midst practitioners of healing and other miracles and wonders; to revive and intensify the practice of bibliomancy (the reading of holy books for the purpose of solving personal problems, or in order to effect some wonder from which one can benefit); and to make their boundaries less porous. These were only tendencies, and not all of them would be in evidence among all groups included in this category. Some of these tendencies can be recognized as already being part of the folk culture. But the folk culture of the earlier centuries was primarily created and cultivated in agrarian settings. The new formations of the early twentieth century faced the opportunities and challenges of the urban worlds. Moreover, higher degrees and more complex types and functions of literacy must be presupposed for the later period and situations.

The groups included in this period have often been called sects. It is worth noting that all African American religious communities have been so labeled for a long period of time by many observers and researchers of American religions. These communities were understood to have been founded in response to, and continue to exist on account of, tensions with the dominant society. It should be clear at this point, however, that this study is in part a response to the inadequacy of such labeling of African American religious communities.

The groups that have generally been dominant within the culture of African American independent churches are the Baptists and Methodists. The origins of these groups lie in earlier periods and should be identified with the previous (third) reading. In terms of numbers and influence, they can certainly be said to have dominated African American religious cultures well into early decades of the twentieth century; they can be classified as part of the dominant religious mainstream within African American communities. But in this fourth reading, the groups that emerge are different.

With a more critical perspective of the world and of American society and its biblical self-understanding, these new groups shared a more fundamental disdain for and mistrust of American society than the Baptists, Methodists, and the segments of African America that they represented. They were less concerned than the more traditional groups about "cashing the check" on America's promise of democracy, equality, and freedom of opportunity. They reflected the strongly felt sentiments of displaced and disoriented rural and small town folks who had migrated to the big cities in search of better economic opportunities and social conditions. The reality experienced by these migrants was mixed: in some cases they found better jobs and greater economic opportunities; some also encountered less legal segregation and strictures. But the situation for the urban majority was decidedly less than utopian. Absence of legal segregation in a few cases did not prevent actual entrenched segregation and virulent, if sometimes veiled, racism in housing patterns, in hiring practices in many industries, and in the financial support given to school systems.[39] The new groups were characterized by their deeper cynicism about American society in general and their criticisms of the older African American religious communities. Cynicism developed on account of society's racism; traditional African communities and their agenda were rejected for their perceived accommodation to the racist society.

The cities, with their larger and more diverse populations, faster pace, greater and more complicated social expectations, greater pressures, rifts and conflicts among all population groups, and especially among minority racial and ethnic groups, provoked the critical attitudes of the new groups. The Black arrivals could hardly avoid being influenced or determined by the forces—quite mixed in their effects—of urban life in the United States from the 1920s through the 1950s. Tremendous population growth in times of limited job growth and limited entrepreneurial, housing, and educational opportunities created pressure and conflicts. Enormous socioeconomic and ideological differentiation existed within the African American population as well. Necessarily, there were many different and conflicting social practices and arrangements among people who had little in common beyond the experience of racism in the larger society. A little social improvement bred some big social problems. Although many among the settled Northerners had beckoned their southern counterparts to come their way for better opportunities, and had welcomed and supported those who did so, others viewed the newcomers with suspicion, alarm, and contempt. After all, they were different—they talked differently, their carriage and pace were different, they worshiped differently.[40]

And while the newcomers seemed to long for more freedom and greater economic opportunities that the North and West seemed to promise, they were loathe to discard all the ways that had marked their lives in the rural south. So they could hardly avoid thinking that many among their northern and western urban counterparts were different. In the mixed urban situation, amid strongly felt perceptions about difference, discord and conflict were inevitable. How should real and lively difference, as opposed to what the ideology of slavery had enforced and maintained, be negotiated? How could it be understood, much less tolerated and negotiated? These were among the challenges facing an increasingly urbanized and diverse African America in the early to middle decades of the twentieth century.[41]

A very different reading of the Bible and of other sacred texts, reflecting the different attitudes about society and culture among the new arrivals, is in evidence from the 1920s through the 1950s and 1960s. It more clearly reflects and articulates the differences in orientation. More to the point, here we confront evidence for a new and different positionality and orientation in African America. It was associated with a number of new formations or associations—the Garvey Movement, Father Divine and the Peace Mission Movement, the Black Jews, the Nation of Islam, the Spiritual churches, and the Pentecostal Movement are among the most prominent ones. What they had in common were sensibilities, attitudes

about the world. These attitudes were reflected not only in their critique and
more radical (Afrocentric or racialist) interpretation of the established Protestant-
defined and -delimited Bible, but also in
their acceptance of other esoteric authoritative texts that, of course, justified their
own different sensibilities and agenda.
Whether through the radical rereadings
of the Protestant Bible, the rejection or
manipulation of its canonical delimita-
tions, or through acceptance of other esoteric authoritative texts, these groups
expressed their rejection of the racist and
worldly religious ways of America and of
the accommodationist and integrationist
agenda of the African American religious
mainstream. Many of them (e.g., the Nation of Islam, the Garvey Movement) focused—to degrees far beyond anything on
record among African American estab-
lishment churches—upon the utter perfidy
of whites and the ultimate salvation and
liberation of African peoples. To articulate their critique and to advance their
own agenda, they drew heavily and with
great creativity either upon their own

special hermeneutical principles or upon special sacred texts.

A dramatic example is Rabbi Matthew, leader of the movement called Black Judaism, which began in Harlem around 1919 and continued for several decades. Rabbi Matthew taught a variant of Ethiopianism. He rejected the claims of white Jews to be the chosen people, and he rejected all the teachings and manifestations of Christianity, including what he perceived to be the misplaced beliefs and practices of African American Christians.

To impugn others and to commend and build his own movement, Rabbi Matthew interpreted the Jewish Bible and other sacred texts and traditions. His reading traced his own movement from antiquity down to its meeting place, its teachings and activities in Harlem on 123rd Street, and of course his own authoritative leadership within the larger scheme of sacred world history:

I must treat briefly the history of the sons of men, from Adam, of whom it is only necessary to say that when

God decided on the necessity of man's existence, He did not choose to make a black man, or a white man: He simply decided to make man . . . from the dust of the earth, in whom he encased the reproductive power of all colors, all species, all shades of all races and eventual nationalities. From Adam to Noah, there were only two classes of men, known as the sons of God and the sons of men . . . a carnal and a spiritual-minded race of the sons of men, both from Adam. The two classes eventually met in Noah and his wife . . . [they] had three sons: Shem, Ham, and Japheth. After the flood Ham took the lead. . . . As Cush rose in power, Africa . . . became the center of the world's cultural and religious education, and thus Ham secured for himself and his posterity for all time, a name—Pioneers of the World's Civilization. After the fall of Cush came Egypt, under Mizri the second son of Ham, into power. He and Shem amalgamated by intermarriage and the Mesopotamians were produced, an interrace between Shem and Ham. . . . They went into Egypt and abode there four hundred and thirty years. They mingled greatly with the Egyptians by intermarriage, and thus Shem and Ham were merged into one great people. . . . All those who had reached maturity before leaving Egypt died in the wilderness except Joshua and Caleb; even Moses . . . died there. But before coming out of Egypt he fled to Median in Ethiopia, only to become servant to the Ethiopian Priest whose daughter he eventually married and begot two sons.

Those two boys were as much Ethiopians as it was possible to be because they were created out of the soil and born in the land, as they were Israelites of the Tribe of Levi, the Priest, because their father was of the tribe of Levi and of the household of Israel. They of necessity had to be black because their father was black, and so was their mother. . . . This great admixture of two great people left Egypt . . . and finally came into the land of

Canaan. Eventually David, son of Jesse of the Tribe of Judah, came to the throne of Israel, and in time his son Solomon succeeded him. When Solomon came to the throne, his fame spread the world over, and to the Queen of Sheba, whose name was Candace Queen of the South. . . . Eventually she became the wife of Solomon, the son that was born to them was Menelik the 1st. The line of the Falashas are counted from Menelik 1st to Menelik the great, who was the uncle of his Imperial Majesty, Haile Selassie, the 1st, the Lion of the Tribe of Judah. It is roughly calculated that before the war there were about a million Falasha Jews in Ethiopia . . . however, since the war they have been greatly reduced, and fear is entertained for their continued existence. In Harlem, N.Y., there are about three thousand adherents to the faith . . . who, with pride, lay claim to this glorious heritage. . . .

It is claimed by these [adherents] that they are among the oldest families of the Jewish or Hebraic race upon the face of the earth, and that they are the only ones to retain their kings to sit upon the Throne of David and, outside of Palestine, to retain the six point star on the money. Our manner and customs are strictly orthodox; we are strictly Koshered. Our children are taught to speak the Hebrew language and to live in keeping with all the commandments of the Almighty. . . . [42]

This reading represents a radically different starting point and set of assumptions from the dominant religious orientation among African Americans. It also represents the significant possibilities for renewal and re-formation. Most pertinent to our discussion is how sacred texts functioned in this effort as fundamental mythic-ideological building blocks in the construction of the new worlds. They represent a discursive-textual field within which mythic-historical origins and new world possibilities and destinies can be articulated.[43] It is their reading of religious texts and other phenomena in general that poignantly reflects these new groups' difference from the older, traditional groups. The new groups' claims to esoteric knowledge and principles of interpretation of holy books corresponded to their rejection of the boundaries that the dominant society and the accommodationist minority communities agreed upon for dialogue and debate about key issues. Outright rejection of the canon itself, or additions to the canon, or esoteric principles of interpretation of whatever canon—these tendencies evidence the radical psychic stance of these groups in relation to the dominant society, the Bible, and other religious texts.

Reading 5

Stepping Outside the Circle: Fundamentalism

The fifth and most recent African American reading of the Bible has to do with fundamentalism and an attraction to white fundamentalist communities. Not unlike the catalysts for the rise of fundamentalist piety among whites in the early decades of this century, the rise of such piety among African Americans in *significant numbers* beginning in the 1940s and 1950s signifies a crisis—of thinking, of security.

White America at the end of the nineteenth century and in the first few decades of the twentieth century was faced with the onslaught of change in every facet of life—the scientific revolution, inventions, a world war and the new awesome weapons it introduced, new questions about reality, and new methods of inquiry designed to address these questions in universities that were becoming more comprehensive and research-oriented. The cumulative change was so great, so radical, that it has been termed a virtual revolution, a "paradigm shift of consciousness."[44]

The shift took different shapes in different contexts at different times. In religious circles, especially among the elites, and in theological seminaries, to be more precise, it began to surface in adoption of new methods of interpreting the Bible. Among many biblical scholars it was no longer assumed that the confessional traditions or the literal rendering of the text was enough to get at its meaning. Historical consciousness required the historical-critical reading of the Bible, understanding it as an ancient document, written in different social contexts and different times by different human authors. Many reacted violently to this new scholarship, branding it as heresy and as an attempt to undermine the authority of the Scriptures and take them away from common folk. The fundamentalist movement was born in reaction. It felt the old, comforting, simple world slipping away and decided that it was necessary to provide a way for common folk to read the Bible that would keep the old world intact yet at the same time speak to some of the difficulties that the new breed of scholars had pointed out. An inductive reading of the texts and a dispensationalist hermeneutic were devised and promoted among the new "Bible-believing" churches, associations, denominations, and academies founded at this time. This response was intended to secure the "fundamentals" of the faith drawn up by the movement against "modernism."[45]

African Americans were not a significant part of the beginnings of the fundamentalist movement in America.[46] Only in recent decades have significant numbers come to embrace fundamentalist ideology and white fundamentalist communities in a self-conscious manner.[47]

Unlike earlier readings, this phenomenon does not seem to reflect the internal politics and the internal criticisms of racialist or culturalist perspectives in general or African Americanist perspectives and traditions in particular. Instead this reading rejects or at least relativizes those perspectives. The intentional attempt to embrace Christian traditions, specifically the attempt to interpret the Bible, without respect for the historical experiences of persons of African descent, radically demarcates this reading and this period from all others.

The growth of fundamentalism among African Americans is evident both in the efforts to change the orientations and rhythms of African American spirituality and churches and in the increase in the number of African Americans who have actually joined white fundamentalist churches and have sent their children to white fundamentalist academies. Those African Americans who actually join white fundamentalist communities have found themselves for the most part having to relativize race and culture as factors in religious faith and piety, and having to argue for the universal nature of the fundamentalist perspective. At the seventeenth annual meeting of the National Black Evangelical Association in 1980, for example, controversy broke out over resignations in leadership provoked by differences of opinion about the theological perspective that should characterize the organization. Although this organization has the reputation for being relatively moderate on theological, social, and political issues, it could not escape having to address the tension between race and culture, on the one hand, and "pure" doctrine, on the other hand. Two divergent views emerged. One maintained that covenant theology, understood as emphasizing God's work in the Black community through history, should be embraced by the association; the other maintained that a strict premillennial and dispensationalist stance was essential. A spokesperson for the second position argued that the association "must rest on the Word, be unified in theology, not culture, color, or history."[48]

There is evidence, then, for the development of a reading of the Bible among African Americans that is different not only from the dominant or mainstream reading (described above, reading 3), but also quite different from the reading of the radicals (also described above, reading 4). In this fifth reading, the Protestant-defined Bible is considered the deracialized, depoliticized, and universal guide to truth and salvation. Radical criticism of African American religious communities and culture is expressed. Insofar as the Protestant canon is not questioned, and insofar as the foundation or presupposition for the reading of the canon is claimed to be something other than African American historical experience as remembered and understood by African Americans, it entails a severe and even disturbing rejection of African American existence.

In much the same way that the rise of fundamentalism among whites in the early decades of the twentieth century represented a rejection of the modernism of so-called white elite culture, so within the world of African Americans a turn toward fundamentalism represents a rejection of the claims about how the shared historical experiences of African Americans should figure in views about religious orientation and practices.[49] It is a most significant development that in religious matters (1) the mainstream and hyper-racialist African American communities have been and continue to be abandoned by some other African Americans allied in different ways with white conservative and fundamentalist camps, (2) that some of these other African American fundamentalist types have either joined or transformed their camps into white fundamentalist camps, and (3) that religious truth can now be claimed to have transcended historical experience. The proliferation of new fundamentalist churches and denominational groups among African Americans; the imitation of the forms, structures, rhetorics and politics of white fundamentalist groups; and the attention, respect, and support given to white media evangelists—these developments are recent and nothing short of astounding. They beg comprehensive investigation and psychosocial and political-ideological explanation.[50]

Accounting for the uses of the Bible among Black "fundamentalists" will require a nuanced understanding of the diversity and differentiation of Black religious communities and of their critical and self-referential language. For example, those who called themselves "Bible believers" implied much about themselves and about all others; they arrogated to themselves a status, level of knowledge, and insight that went far beyond what was claimed in most African American groups. Such criticisms and claims seemed different; they reflected not only a different set of ideas and a different orientation, but also a different kind of claim about spirituality.

The origins of such orientations and formations are obscure. According to A. G. Miller, the founding of many African American evangelical and fundamentalist "Bible-believing" churches and associations was spurred by what is sometimes termed the African American Bible School movement of the 1920s through the 1950s and with the founding of a few Bible colleges in such places as Dallas, Atlanta, New York, and Florida. These churches and associated institutions were founded and led first by evangelical and fundamentalist whites who reportedly worked in the interest of bringing the truth about the "true Word" to African Americans. Like the mainstream African American churches, schools, and colleges that, in their early years were also sponsored and led by white churches and religious organizations before Blacks assumed leadership roles, the fundamentalist African American schools and churches were first led by whites, then subsequently led by ideologically and theologically appropriate African Americans.[51]

Although the numbers of African American churches that have formal affiliations with white evangelical and fundamentalist groups may be relatively small, the influence of such groups upon African American churches and individuals must not be underestimated. In the movement's early years the constant cry among clergy and laypersons for training in the Bible and related subjects and the aggressive and integrated missionary agenda and tactics in the Bible school culture did not result in dramatic growth in the enrollment of African American churches within the white fundamentalist camps. But the few enrolled churches and their relationships with schools made the influence powerful in the long run. The single-minded, single-issue Bible schools proved to be quite significant as ideological-rhetorical training and recruitment camps in ways that few other schools contemplated or were allowed.[52]

But what is most significant about the development of African American fundamentalism is that it represents using the Bible as a weapon in a broad criticism of African American culture. The sharp criticism of the biblical illiteracy of African Americans is actually quite incredible. Rather than seeing in such criticism a mere reference to the lack of a certain type of education, or knowledge of the pertinent "facts," it should be interpreted as a radical religious resocialization. It amounts to a deracialization of the African American religious world view, masked, of course, as a legitimate, authoritative, and broad-based, if not universal, race-neutral view and stance. To understand clearly what developed, one needs to see the necessary negative correlation that was set up. Protestant-defined fundamentalism, with its obvious racial, ethnic, and class origins, was masked as a movement that had transcended all such categories through its fetishization of the Bible as text. As this fundamentalism was embraced by African Americans, African American historical cultural experiences were (depending upon the particular strain of fundamentalism or the nature of outside pressures) necessarily backgrounded, rendered invisible, or held in contempt.

Some of the psychological and cultural-political effects of white fundamentalist culture—especially as inculated by the Bible schools—on African Americans can be noted in the perspective provided by William E. Pannell. A long-time pastor, senior leader, and mentor of many

Black self-styled evangelicals and funda-
mentalists, as well as a professor at Fuller
Seminary in California, Pannell reflected
back upon his years as a young African
American male in attendance at the Fort
Wayne Bible School:

> Bible College opened up a whole new
> world. It also narrowed considerably
> the old one. . . . Gradually, and with-
> out any conscious realization, the
> world got smaller too. We were taught
> to shun the world, to be separate from
> it, and while I am sure the interest
> was right, the result of such instruc-
> tion developed a negative and defen-
> sive mentality. . . . I became a
> fundamentalist. . . . Orthodoxy was
> all-important and at times even love
> for those who differed was considered
> compromise, betrayal or apostasy. The
> same could be said, of course, for my
> contemporaries in liberal schools.
> From our deep wells we fought our
> verbal battles, never caring that we
> were strangers to the love of God.[53]

Pannell's understanding of his experience is poignant. Clearly the type of experience he describes has had and continues to have significant psychosocial, socio-cultural, and political effects. Acceptance of the practices and politics of (white) fundamentalism would seem to demand in principle a type or degree of self-emptying, self-questioning, self-loathing, and self-contempt, all experienced on the superficial level as a certain construal of piety.[54] That the same assessment may be made of African Americans' engagements of other forms of white religious and other traditions is clear enough. But notwithstanding failings and inconsistencies of some of these other traditions, they seem not to be defined by the principled erasure or negation of African American traditions.

Reading 6

Making the Circle True: Women's Experiences

In evidence throughout this history of African American readings of the Bible are the readings of African American women. From Phillis Wheatley to modern womanist and other interpreters not known by name, women have been full participants in—that is, have helped define and set the limits of—each of the readings distinguished above. But across each of these readings, differences in historical periods, locations, classes, and other factors notwithstanding, collectively women have added a special emphasis. Although it is clear that African American women have always spoken forcefully and eloquently about themselves and the pertinent issues of their times, they have expressed a common theme or sentiment about women, which is brought out most dramatically in readings of the Bible. Poignantly and ironically, the most acute challenge associated with women's readings has to do with raised consciousness about and efforts to work toward realizing the ideal of inclusion of all—with special emphasis on females—in positions of authority, leadership, and responsibility within African American society and culture, including religious communities. The ever-elusive historical realization of this ideal among African American women—even as African Americans have partly found their prophetic voice and stance in relation to dominant white culture on the basis of the same sort of challenge—has inspired African American women's voices in notes and refrains different from their male counterparts. Thus, most of the public readings identified above can be defined as mostly although not exclusively *male* readings.

The common theme or sentiment regarding radical inclusion among male readers notwithstanding, African Ameri-

can women have come to expression
about the topic in very different ways. It
is in light of the dominance of men—including Black men, in decidedly fewer
numbers and to far lesser degrees, of
course—in traditional society, especially
on the public stage and forum, that
women's expression should be seen. To be
sure, women have historically had less
access to the public stage and forum, but
they have nonetheless come to expression in different genres and media, such
as in journals and diaries; some in artistic
works, such as poetry, fiction and music;
others in public speeches, including sermons; still others in scholarly works.[55]
Women's different positionality, then, has
forced them and allowed them to "read"
the struggle for equality and inclusion
differently—more insistently and consistently, more poignantly and radically.

The Bible has figured prominently in
this struggle. As they have engaged the
Bible, African American women have generally assumed that it privileges women's
interests insofar as women's presence and
participation in different social and cul-

tural settings, including religious settings, are seen as the dramatic index of the inclusion, acceptance, and dignity of all. Understood as *radical* inclusion, acceptance, and empowerment, women's presence and participation in the world are seen as having been ordained by God and modeled in biblical stories. That such presence and participation have historically been controversial only helps bolster the claim about its biblical origins and divine mandate.

Nineteenth-century charismatic preacher Jarena Lee is an important and well-known example of an African American woman who seemed very much aware of the implications and ramifications of interpreting the Bible specifically with a view to establishing clarity about God's calling of women to do important tasks in the world:

Did not Mary first preach the risen Saviour, and is not the doctrine of the resurrection the very climax of Christianity—hangs not all our hope on this, as argued by St. Paul? Then did not Mary, a woman, preach the gospel?

But some will say that Mary did not expound the Scripture, therefore, she did not preach, in the proper sense of the term. To this I reply, it may be that the term *preach* in those primitive times, did not mean exactly what it is now made to mean; perhaps, it was a great deal more simple then, than it is now—if it were not, the unlearned fishermen could not have preached the gospel at all, as they had no learning.

To this it may be replied, by those who are determined not to believe that it is right for a woman to preach, that the disciples, though they were fishermen and ignorant of letters too, were inspired so to do . . . though they were inspired, yet that inspiration did not save them from showing their ignorance of letters, and of man's wisdom; this the multitude soon found out. . . . If then, to preach the gospel, by the gist of heaven, comes by inspiration solely, is God straitened: must he take the man exclusively? May he not, did he not, and can he not inspire a female to preach the simple story of the birth, life, death, and resurrection of our Lord, and accompany it too with power to the sinner's heart? As for me, I am fully persuaded that the Lord called me to labor according to what I have received in his vineyard. If he has not, how could he consistently bear testimony in favor of my poor labors, in awakening and converting sinners?[56]

Among the many fascinating aspects of this excerpt from Lee's autobiographical narrative is the critical thinking she evidences about the controversy around women's calling from God and the right and responsibility to preach God's truth. The controversy about her ministerial presence and participation, her rights and authority, seems to have inspired Lee to think about radical marginality and disprivilege and to associate herself with those of the lowest social status. As is made hauntingly clear from the excerpt, this association and thinking do not lead to self-loathing, self-abjection, and to acceptance of marginalization and disprivilege, but to the eloquent arrogation of her rights and authority within the circles led by men, most especially those men of her own race, claiming to be formed by God. Her calling was among other things to enlarge such a circle and make it true.

Ongoing Engagement

The Bible has held the most prominent place in shaping the forms and content of the African American imaginary. This role should not surprise. The Bible was on one level easily at hand for world re-formation as part of the larger European cultural, rhetorical, and imaginative repertoire. Among the African slaves and former slaves it was drawn upon with intensity. This intensity is to be accounted for by the acute suffering and pain that has marked African existence in the North Atlantic worlds. But clearly the matter was not left with pain and suffering. The people's history with the Bible also reflects agency and social power. The Bible was embraced and continues to be embraced to help build other worlds of language, discourse, and imagination within an already more broadly biblically constructed world that is the West in general, and the United States in particular. These African American worlds are constituted by circles of readings within which peoples whose voice had been taken away were able to speak again— about themselves and all the things they encounter. Through such speaking they were positioned to find ways, as Toni Morrison put it, to "re-memory"[57] the pain that has defined the past and use it to make and sustain circles of social power.

Many questions and issues remain. It is clear that not all African Americans have embraced the Bible. It is also clear that not all of those who have embraced it have been able to realize and sustain the empowerment it has promised. Clearer still is that the meaning of the text (that is, the Bible) is not itself the issue. It is not the meaning *of* the text but meaning *and* text that are at issue. It is the more complex phenomenon of *engagement*—the collective consciousness being threaded through, changing, and being changed by the Bible over time—that has been decisive and should therefore be the focus of serious and sensitive study. The history of African Americans' engagements with the Bible is compelling because it is the history of those whose experiences in the West represent and force a dramatic lag,[58] an interruption that can open wide a window onto a deeper understanding of what, in the great range of possibilities and problems, it has meant and may still mean to engage Scriptures.

Notes

1. See Henri Desroche, *Sociology of Hope,* trans. Carol Martin-Sperry (London: Routledge & Kegan Paul, 1979), for discussion of the sociopolitical effectiveness of the imaginary.

2. See Charles H. Long, *Significations: Signs, Symbols, and Images in the Interpretation of Religion* (Philadelphia: Fortress Press, 1986), for discussion of the term in relationship to African Americans.

3. This concept is developed by Orlando Patterson in *Slavery and Social Death: A Comparative Study* (Cambridge: Harvard University Press, 1982).

4. See Donald G. Mathews, *Religion in the Old South* (Chicago: University of Chicago Press, 1977), 136, for discussion of various perceptions (and of pertinent primary sources).

5. See John Thornton, *Africa and Africans in the Making if the Atlantic World, 1400–1800,* Studies in Comparative World History, 2d ed.

(Cambridge: Cambridge University Press, 1998); Jean Comaroff and John Comaroff, *Of Revelation and Revolution: Christianity, Colonialism, and Consciousness in South Africa,* vol. 1 (Chicago: University of Chicago Press, 1991); *idem., Ethnography and the Historical Imagination: Studies in the Ethnographic Imagination* (Boulder, Colo.: Westview, 1991); and Sylvia R. Frey and Betty Wood, *Come Shouting to Zion: African American Protestantism in the American South and British Caribbean to 1830* (Chapel Hill: University of North Carolina Press, 1998) for discussions of issues and pertinent primary sources.

6. See on this point the extended discussion in Comaroff and Comaroff, *Of Revelation and Revolution,* chaps. 2 and 3 on the South African situation.

7. Ibid., chap. 6, esp. 213, 218, 228f., 236f., 245f.

8. Ibid., chap. 5, descriptions of first encounters.

9. See description (unfortunately, with little certainly questionable analysis if any) of some selected perceptions and reactions in H. W. Turner, *Religious Innovation in Africa: Collected Essays on New Religious Movements* (Boston: Hall, 1979) 271–88. Note also the many works by Jack Goody

on literacy and orality, including the most recent collection of essays, *The Power of the Written Word* (Washington, D.C.: Smithsonian Institute, 2000).

10. Thornton, *Africa and Africans,* 248–50.

11. Adam Jones, ed. and trans., *German Sources for West African History, 1599-1669* (Wiesbaden: Steiner, 1983), 91. See also Thornton's discussion (*Africa and Africans,* 251) of the incident that provoked the different perceptions.

12. Comaroff and Comaroff, *Of Revelation and Revolution,* 243f.

13. See Mathews, *Religion in the Old South,* 198f.; and Lawrence W. Levine, B*lack Culture and Black Consciousness* (New York: Oxford University Press, 1977), 136f.

14. See the illuminating essays in Nathan O. Hatch and Mark A. Noll, eds., *The Bible in America: Essays in Cultural History* (New York : Oxford University Press, 1982).

15. See Albert J. Raboteau, *Slave Religion: The "Invisible Institution" in the Antebellum South* (New York: Oxford University Press, 1978), 239f.; and Mathews, *Religion in the Old South,* 212–36.

16. See James Weldon Johnson, ed., *The Book of American Negro Spirituals* (New York: Viking Press, 1925), 20, 21.

17. Among the many treatments now available, see: Bryan R. Wilson, *Magic and the Millennium: A Sociological Study of Religious Movements of Protest among Tribal and Third World Peoples* (New York: Harper & Row, 1973); Malcom B. Hamilton, *The Sociology of Religion: Theoretical and Comparative Perspectives* (London: Routledge, 1995); Thomas F. O'Dea, *The Sociology of Religion,* Foundations of Modern Sociology series (Englewood Cliff, N.J.: Prentice Hall, 1966); and Sumner B. Twiss and Walter H. Conser, eds., *The Experience of the Sacred: Readings in the Phenomenology of Religion* (Hanover, N.H.: University Press of New England, 1992).

18. There are too few studies on African Americans and their religions in this disciplinary area. But see now Hans A. Singer and Merill Singer, *African-American Religion in the Twentieth Century: Varieties of Protest and Accommodation* (Knoxville: University of Tennessee Press, 1992); the well-received work of the late Walter Pitts, *Old Ship of Zion: The Afro-Baptist Ritual in the African Diaspora* (New York: Oxford University Press, 1993); and Anthony B. Pinn's *Varieties of African American Religious Experience* (Minneapolis: Fortress Press, 1998).

19. That the songs and sermons reflect a type

of indirect or veiled commentary on the social situation that the African slaves faced has been noted by most interpreters. In addition to Johnson, *The Book of American Negro Spirituals,* see also the classic interpretations by Howard Thurman, *Deep River and the Negro Spiritual Speaks of Life and Death* (Richmond, Ind.: Friends United Press, 1975) and Benjamin E. Mays, *The Negro's God as Reflected in His Literature* (New York: Atheneum, 1969). But more careful attention to the manner in which the images and language of the Bible were used can shed more light on the question of the oppositional character of African American religion. See James H. Cone, *Black Theology and Black Power* (San Francisco: Harper & Row, 1989); Gayraud Wilmore, *Black Religion and Black Radicalism: An Interpretation of the Religious History of African Americans* (Maryknoll, N.Y.: Orbis, 1998); and the more recent work of Dwight N. Hopkins, *Down, Up, and Over: Slave Religion and Black Theology* (Minneapolis: Fortress Press, 2000). I would argue that studying the selection of biblical texts/stories and their redaction by these early African Americans can force entirely different and more illuminating categories upon the discussion. Attention to both biblical story and African American redaction will

more likely bring into focus the major emphases
and concerns of the African Americans who sang,
prayed, and testified in the language of the Bible.
Detailed exegetical treatments of the raw materials of the African cultural-historical experiences
and expressions of this period are in order. More
specifically, comparative or redaction-critical
studies of biblical text/stories in relation to
African American stories drawn from the Bible
are needed.

20. See Zora Neale Hurston, *Mules and Men*
(New York: Harper Perennial, 1990), 33, 218.

21. Ibid., 3.

22. Ibid., 125.

23. Ibid., 224.

24. Ibid., 208.

25. See Newbell Puckett, *Folk Beliefs of the
Southern Negro* (Chapel Hill: University of North
Carolina Press, 1926), 568

26. See ibid., chaps. 3–5. See also Theophus H.
Smith, *Conjuring Culture: Biblical Formations of
Black America* (New York: Oxford University
Press, 1998), for a less strictly historical interpre-
tive but more nuanced cultural-critical, philosoph-
ical, and theological development of the topic.

27. Here it is important to take seriously the
provocative work of anthropologist Grey Gun-

daker. In *Signs of Diaspora, Diaspora of Signs: Literacies, Creolization, and Vernacular Practice in America* (New York: Oxford University Press, 1998), she argues that African Americans' relationship to traditional scripts and literacy is complex and layered and should not be seen simply in terms of oral versus literate traditions and orientations.

28. See Donald E. Pease, ed., *National Identities and Post-American Narratives* (Durham: Duke University Press, 1994) for a collection of essays on historical and comparative perspectives on the formation of (U.S.) national identities.

29. See Timothy E. Fulop and Albert J. Raboteau, eds., *African-American Religion: Interpretive Essays in History and Culture* (New York: Routledge, 1997); James M. Washington, *Frustrated Fellowship: The Black Baptist Quest for Social Power* (Macon, Ga.: Mercer University Press, 1987); C. Eric Lincoln and Lawrence Mamiya, eds., *The Black Church in the African American Experience* (Durham, N.C.: Duke University Press, 1990); Milton C. Sernett, ed., *African American Religious History: A Documentary Witness*, 2d ed. (Durham N.C.: Duke University Press, 1999).

30. See Wilmore, *Black Religion and Black Radicalism*, chap. 6, for provocative development of the topic.

31. See Martin E. Marty, *Religion and Republic: The American Circumstance* (Boston: Beacon, 1987), 140–65.

32. See Peter J. Paris, *The Social Teaching of the Black Churches* (Philadelphia: Fortress, Press, 1985), for discussion.

33. Cited in Paris, *Social Teaching,* 13.

34. Ibid., 51

35. Cited in Sernett, *African American Religious History,* 107–8. Frederick Douglass's excoriations of the white Christianity of his time are threaded through his critical reading of Jesus' words to his disciples about contemporary Jewish leaders in Jerusalem ("scribes and Pharisees") as rendered in Matt. 23:4, 5.

36. Cited in Sterling Stuckey, ed., *The Ideological Origins of Black Nationalism* (Boston: Beacon, 1972), 44–45, 54. Obviously, there are ranges of perspectives and agenda within Black nationalism—in the nineteenth century and in our own times—as Stuckey makes clear. See also Wilmore, *Black Religion and Black Radicalism,* chap. 5; and Robin D. G. Kelley and Sidney Lemelle, *Imagining Home: Class, Culture, and Nationalism in the African Diaspora* (New York: Verso, 1994).

37. Quotation taken from Marilyn Richardson, ed., *Maria W. Stewart, America's First Black Woman Political Writer: Essays and Speeches*

(Bloomington: Indiana University Press, 1987), 63, 64.

38. See Milton C. Sernett's *Bound for the Promised Land: African American Religion and the Great Migration* (Durham, N.C.: Duke University Press, 1997), for a very informative and singular treatment of the religious impulses behind the Great Migration. For a different but not necessarily antithetical perspective, see Robin D. G. Kelley and Earl Lewis, *To Make Our World Anew: A History of African Americans* (New York: Oxford University Press, 2000).

39. See Lincoln and Mamiya, eds., *The Black Church,* chap 6.

40. See on this matter artist Jacob Lawrence's interpretation of the phenomenon of migration, including his view of the reception that some Northerners gave to the newly arrived Southerners. See Peter T. Nesbett and Michelle Dubois, eds., *Over the Line: The Art and Life of Jacob Lawrence* (Seattle: University of Washington Press, 2000).

41. See the fascinating essays collected and edited by Robert Orsi, *Gods of the City: Religion and the Urban Landscape* (Bloomington Ind.: Indiana University Press, 1999) regarding some of the challenges facing mixed urban populations at a later time.

42. From Sernett, *African American Religious History*, 473–75.

43. See Wesley A. Kort's discussion of this topic in *"Take, Read": Scripture, Textuality, and Cultural Practice* (University Park, Pa.: Pennsylvania State University Press, 1996), 2f.

44. See Timothy P. Weber's development of this argument in "The Two-Edged Sword: The Fundamentalist Use of the Bible," in *The Bible in America: Essays in Cultural History*, ed., Nathan O. Hatch and Mark A. Noll (New York: Oxford University Press, 1982), 101–20.

45. Ibid., 113–14.

46. George M. Marsden, *Fundamentalism and American Culture: The Shaping of Twentieth Century Evangelicalism: 1870–1925* (New York: Oxford University Press, 1980), 228.

47. Of course, exceptions can always be found. What I have in mind here is the historical importance of the shared experience of the legacy of slavery and continuing racial oppression as a buffer against embracing unmixed American Protestant-style fundamentalism, with its principles against explicit naming of self and location in relation to truth claims.

48. Anthony T. Evans, quoted in Jimmy Locklear, "Theology–Culture Rift Surfaces among

Black Evangelicals," *Christianity Today* 24 (May 23, 1980): 44. Most important here is the occurrence of a rift of the sort named. With this issue in mind, the ministries and publications of the likes of evangelist Tom Skinner are certainly worth serious and sensitive study.

49. Among the several studies on the subject that have been published in the last several decades, I have found especially helpful and illuminating Kathleen C. Boone's *The Bible Tells Them So: The Discourse of Protestant Fundamentalism* (Albany, N.Y.: State University of New York Press, 1988).

50. Consider, for example, the many stories passed along about African American ancestors' refusal to believe that certain teachings—namely, acceptance of slavery—were really in the Bible. (The story about theologian Howard Thurman's grandmother is probably the best-known version. But a perusal of folk stories will establish that the attitude is widespread.) Given their circumstances—illiteracy, poverty, being objects of racial hatred—their refusal should be understood to have been based as much upon their critical and willful skepticism about the legitimacy of white folks' translations of the truth as about any speculation about what they thought was in the Bible. At any

rate, this type of historically broadly shared disposition among the "folk" is what seems so far removed from the orientations of fundamentalism. This transformation of consciousness and disposition should be given far more attention in studies on African American religious history.

51. A. G. Miller, "The Construction of a Black Fundamentalist Worldview: The Role of Bible Schools," in Vincent L. Wimbush, ed., *African Americans and the Bible: Sacred Texts and Social Textures* (New York: Continuum, 2000) 712–27.

52. Ibid., 717f.

53. William E. Pannell, *My Friend, the Enemy* (Waco, Tx.: Word Book, 1986), cited by Miller, "The Construction of a Black Fundamentalist Worldview," 718.

54. I am aware that there are diverse views and expressions about these matters in the camps. But it is enough for my purposes to establish that there are views of the sort indicated in the quotation.

55. For resources, see: Henry Louis Gates Jr., ed., *Schomburg Library of Nineteenth-Century Black Women Writers* (New York: Oxford University Press, 1988–); Bettye Collier-Thomas, ed., *Daughters of Thunder: Black Women Preachers and Their Sermons* (San Francisco: Jossey-Bass,

1997); Carla L. Peterson, ed., *"Doers of the Word": African-American Women Speakers and Writers in the North (1830–1880)* (New York: Oxford University Press, 1995); and Richard J. Douglass-Chin, ed., *Preacher Woman Sings the Blues: The Autobiographies of Nineteenth-Century African American Evangelists* (Columbia: University of Missouri Press, 2001).

56. Sue E. Houchins, Introduction to *Spiritual Narratives: Schomburg Library of Nineteenth-Century Black Women Writers,* ed. Henry Louis Gates (New York: Oxford University Press,1988), 11–12.

57. See Toni Morrison's development of this concept in her novel *Beloved* (New York: Penguin Books, 2000). Compare also Homi K. Bhabha's discussion in *The Location of Culture* (New York: Routledge, 1994), 198, 254; and the collection of interpretive essays in William L. Andrews and Nellie Y. McKay, eds., *Toni Morison's Beloved: A Casebook* (New York: Oxford University Press, 1999).

58. Bhabha, *The Location of Culture,* 191, 199.